science for a changing world

Prepared in cooperation with the Bureau of Reclamation

Bull Trout Forage Investigations in Beulah Reservoir, Oregon—Annual Report for 2006

By Brien P. Rose and Mathew G. Mesa

Open-File Report 2009-1036

U.S. Department of the Interior
U.S. Geological Survey

U.S. Department of the Interior
KEN SALAZAR, Secretary

U.S. Geological Survey
Suzette M. Kimball, Acting Director

U.S. Geological Survey, Reston, Virginia: 2009

For more information on the USGS—the Federal source for science about the Earth, its natural and
living resources, natural hazards, and the environment, visit http://www.usgs.gov or call 1-888-ASK-USGS.
For an overview of USGS information products, including maps, imagery, and publications,
visit *http://www.usgs.gov/pubprod*

To order this and other USGS information products, visit *http://store.usgs.gov*

Suggested citation:
Rose, B.P., and Mesa, M.G., 2009, Bull trout forage investigations in Beulah Reservoir, Oregon—Annual report for
2006: U.S. Geological Survey Open-File Report 2009-1036, 38 p.

Contents

Figures

Tables

Conversion Factors, Acronyms, Abbreviations, and Symbols

SI to Inch/Pound

Multiply	By	To obtain
Length		
centimeter (cm)	0.3937	inch (in.)
millimeter (mm)	0.03937	inch (in.)
meter (m)	3.281	foot (ft)
kilometer (km)	0.6214	mile (mi)
Area		
square meter (m^2)	0.0002471	acre
Volume		
liter (L)	0.2642	gallon (gal)
cubic kilometer (km^3)	0.2399	cubic mile (mi^3)
cubic meter (m^3)	0.0008107	acre-foot (acre-ft)
Mass		
gram (g)	0.03527	ounce, avoirdupois (oz)

Temperature in degrees Celsius (°C) may be converted to degrees Fahrenheit (°F) as follows:
°F=(1.8×°C)+3
Concentrations of chemical constituents in water are given either in milligrams per liter (mg/L) or micrograms per liter (µg/L).

Acronyms, Abbreviations, and Symbols

BOR	Bureau of Reclamation
CPUE	catch per unit effort
DO	dissolved oxygen
FL	fork length
h	hour
<	less than
min	minute
>	more than
NFMR	North Fork Malheur River
USFWS	U.S. Fish and Wildlife Service
USGS	U.S. Geological Survey
SD	standard deviation

Bull Trout Forage Investigations in Beulah Reservoir, Oregon—Annual Report for 2006

By Brien P. Rose and Mathew G. Mesa

Abstract

Beulah Reservoir on the north fork of the Malheur River in northeastern Oregon provides irrigation water to nearby farms and ranches and supports an adfluvial population of bull trout (*Salvelinus confluentus*), which are listed as threatened under the Endangered Species Act. Water management in Beulah Reservoir results in seasonal and annual fluctuations of water volume that may affect forage availability for bull trout. Because no minimum pool requirements currently exist, the reservoir is occasionally reduced to run-of-river levels, which may decimate forage fish populations and ultimately affect bull trout. We sampled fish and aquatic insects in Beulah Reservoir in the spring, before the annual drawdown of 2006, and afterward, in the late fall. We also collected samples 1.5 years after the reservoir was dewatered for three consecutive summers. Overall, the moderate drawdown of 2006 (32 percent of full pool) did not drastically alter the fish community in Beulah Reservoir. We did document, however, decreases in abundance and sizes of chironomids in areas of the reservoir that were frequently dewatered, increased catch rates of fish with gillnets, and decreases in population estimates for smaller fishes after drawdown. In 2006, after the dewaterings of 2002–04, species composition was similar to that prior to the dewaterings, but the size distributions of most species were biased toward small juvenile or subyearling fishes and larger fishes were rare. Our results indicate that repeated reservoir drawdown reduces aquatic insect forage for bull trout and probably affects forage fish populations at least temporarily. The high catch rates of juvenile fishes 1.5 years after consecutive dewaterings suggests good reproductive success for any remaining adult fish, and shows that the fish community in Beulah Reservoir is resilient to such disturbances. There is, however, a period of time after serious drawdowns before significant numbers of juvenile fishes start to appear in the reservoir. Because Beulah Reservoir experiences a wide variety of drawdown scenarios in consecutive years, the forage fish community may never reach a state of equilibrium.

Introduction

In 1998, Bull trout (*Salvelinus confluentus*) were listed by the United States Fish and Wildlife Service (USFWS) as a threatened species under the Endangered Species Act throughout the Columbia River and Klamath River basins. Populations of bull trout are in decline throughout their range, and the State of Oregon has listed the North Fork Malheur River (NFMR) population as one "of special concern." As a result, managers have spent considerable time and effort identifying, restoring, and preserving critical habitat and various life history forms of bull trout (Muhlfeld and others, 2003). Reasons for the decline of the bull trout in the Malheur River basin include habitat degradation and fragmentation, losses through unscreened diversions, historical chemical treatment projects (Ratliff and Howell, 1992) and entrainment through Agency Valley Dam on the NFMR.

Beulah Reservoir, which was formed by the Bureau of Reclamation's (BOR) Agency Valley Dam, currently supports an adfluvial population of bull trout that over-winter in the reservoir from November through early May (Gonzalez, 1998; Schwabe and Tiley, 1999). Similar over-wintering behavior of adfluvial bull trout has been documented in Flathead Lake, Montana, and Lake Billy Chinook, Oregon (Fraley and Shepard, 1989; Beauchamp and Van Tassell, 2001). Because the reservoir provides irrigation water to nearby farms and ranches, bull trout in the reservoir can be subjected to changes in water level, habitat, and forage availability due to seasonal and annual reservoir drawdowns. Reservoir volume occasionally decreases to run-of-river levels, which could adversely affect forage fish populations. Decreased forage fish populations could in turn negatively affect the bull trout population within the NFMR drainage by contributing to decreased growth and survival.

Understanding the resilience of the aquatic community in Beulah Reservoir to drawdown and occasional dewatering is important for assessing the impacts of reservoir operations to bull trout. Generally, open systems like streams and rivers are considered resilient to disturbances such as severe drought (Bayley and Osborne, 1993) and flooding (Matthews, 1986). Such resilience is likely due to large numbers of individuals in nearby tributaries or reaches that can quickly re-colonize disturbed areas (Mathews, 1986; Bayley and Osborne, 1993). In contrast, reservoir fish communities may be more confined and potentially less resilient to environmental disturbance. Drastic or ill-timed changes in water levels of reservoirs can lead to the dewatering of spawning habitat, eggs, and larval fishes (Lantz and others, 1967; Estes, 1972), reduced growth and survival of fishes (Graham and others, 1981), and changes in aquatic vegetation, water chemistry, primary production, or the benthic food web (Benson and Hudson, 1975; Nichols, 1975; Woods and Falter, 1982; Gaboury and Patalas, 1984; Furey and others, 2006). Information on the resilience of the aquatic community in Beulah Reservoir to water level changes would be useful for the management of threatened bull trout.

The USFWS and the BOR recently completed a biological opinion that addressed terms and conditions to minimize the effects of Beulah Reservoir operations on bull trout. These terms, and other information, establish conservation pool requirements based on water year conditions that supply adequate habitat and forage for bull trout in the reservoir. To assist in this endeavor, we participated in a cooperative study with the BOR, and addressed the following objectives in our first year of work: (1) document species composition, abundance, and distribution of forage fish in Beulah Reservoir in early spring and late fall, before and after summer drawdown, (2) describe seasonal variation in aquatic insect abundance and distribution, and (3) compare metrics between seasons and from results of sampling in previous years. We propose to use this information to evaluate the resiliency of the aquatic community in Beulah Reservoir to typical seasonal drawdowns and to more drastic events, such as the complete dewatering of the reservoir in 2002, 2003, and 2004. We plan to eventually combine information on forage fish populations with bioenergetics modeling of bull trout consumption and growth to help develop minimum pool recommendations that will provide bull trout with sufficient forage in high, medium, and low water years.

Description of Site and Study Methods

Study site.—Agency Valley Dam was constructed on the NFMR during 1934-35 at river km 29 and formed Beulah Reservoir (fig. 1). The impoundment is managed by the BOR and provides irrigation water to local farms and some flood control. Upstream or downstream passage of fish was terminated upon completion of the dam. The reservoir is 1,020 m above sea level at full pool and has an average width of 1.9 km and a length of about 4 km. The NFMR and Warm Springs Creek enter from the north and the NFMR exits from the south end of the reservoir. The north end of the reservoir is relatively shallow (< 10 m deep) with a low gradient bottom. At the south end of the reservoir, the bottom drops quickly from shore and reaches a maximum depth of about 23 m. Although summer temperatures exceed 20°C at all depths throughout the reservoir (Petersen and others, 2003), it cools rapidly in the fall and typically ices over in the winter. Beulah Reservoir is eutrophic (Bureau of Reclamation, 2002), with high abundances and diverse size classes of redside shiners (*Richardsonius balteatus*), redband rainbow trout (RBT; *Oncorhynchus mykiss*), suckers (*Catostomus spp.*), and northern pikeminnow (*Ptychocheilus oregonensis*; Petersen and others, 2003). The reservoir is stocked each spring with hatchery RBT.

Water-quality sampling.—We collected water quality data (and sampled fish and aquatic insect populations) in Beulah Reservoir during the spring (April through mid-June) and fall (October through mid-November) of 2006. Water temperature, dissolved oxygen (DO), and water transparency were measured about every two weeks in three areas of the reservoir: (1) the deep, southern end; (2) the moderately deep, middle of the reservoir; and (3) the shallow northern end. Dissolved oxygen (mg/L) and water temperature (°C) were measured at depth intervals of 1 m from the surface to the bottom with a Yellow Springs Instruments Model 85 multi-meter. Reservoir transparency was determined with a Secchi disk.

Aquatic-insect sampling.—We estimated the density of pelagic macroinvertebrates in the reservoir using a 0.5-m 2, 500-µm mesh conical zooplankton net towed vertically from about 1 m above the bottom to the water surface. During the spring and fall, we conducted three net tows from randomly selected sites within each of four geographic areas (i.e., northwest, northeast, southwest, and southeast) of the reservoir and combined catches into four composite samples by area. Samples were preserved in the field with 70 percent ethanol. In the laboratory, organisms were identified to Order and the number and total weight (blotted dry) were recorded. Mean weights of individuals were calculated by dividing total number of insects per sample by their combined weight. Samples were averaged to estimate aquatic insect density and biomass for the reservoir.

We also estimated the abundance and biomass of benthic insects in three shoreline and bottom strata that experience different magnitudes of dewatering, including areas that were: (1) frequently dewatered [> 1,010-m elevation, about 25 percent of reservoir depths, and dewatered in 84 – 100 percent of the years between 1977-2005]; (2) occasionally dewatered [from 997-1,010-m or about 63 percent of reservoir depths and dewatered in 14 – 83 percent of the previous 28 years]; or (3) usually not dewatered [< 997-m elevation or about 13 percent of reservoir depths and < 14 percent of previous years] during typical summer drawdown. We collected two samples of benthic invertebrates from random locations within these strata using a Ponar dredge during the spring when the reservoir was nearly full. We repeated this process every 2-4 weeks and processed samples as described above.

Fish sampling.—Fish were sampled about every other week in the spring and fall with experimental gill and fyke nets. The gill nets were 36.5 m long by 3.0 m deep and contained six 6-m panels with stretch mesh sizes of 8.9, 7.6, 6.3, 5.1, 3.8, and 2.5 cm. Gill nets were generally fished on the bottom during daylight hours for 30 min or less. Fyke nets (91-cm-high, 122-cm-wide, and 0.6-cm # 44 mesh) were set with a 13-m center lead extending to shore and fished overnight. We used a stratified (by the four geographic areas of the reservoir) randomized design to establish sampling locations for each gear type with sample sites replaced at the start of each session. Captured fish were lightly anesthetized (non-game fish and bull trout: 50 mg/L buffered MS-222; game fish: one tablet of Alka-Seltzer Gold© in 2.5 L of water), identified to species (except for sculpins), measured (fork length [FL] in mm), weighed (only a sub-sample to the nearest 0.1 g), marked by clipping a fin (juvenile fish) or placing a Floy tag in the dorsal musculature (fish > 150 mm), and released. Later, we estimated the weights of individuals that were not weighed using the length-weight relation derived from fish that we did weigh. When fish numbers precluded us from processing fish in a timely manner, we sub-sampled about 500 individuals per fyke net and counted the remaining young-of-the-year fishes.

We estimated the population abundance and total biomass for the most common species and ages of fish (i.e., young-of-the-year and adult) in the spring and fall using the Schumacher-Eschmeyer estimator for multiple census mark-recapture studies (Schneider, 1998). We assumed compliance with all assumptions associated with this estimator [see Lagler (1956) for a summary]. Biomass estimates for each species were generated by multiplying the average weight of fish in each cohort by their estimated population size.

Stomach contents were collected from all bull trout using non-lethal gastric lavage and preserved in 10 percent buffered formalin. In the laboratory, organisms were identified to the lowest practical taxon and the number and total weight (blotted dry) were recorded.

Water quality, insect, and fish response to reservoir drawdown.—To examine the effects of a typical summer drawdown on the aquatic community in Beulah Reservoir, we compared several metrics between seasons from our sampling in 2006. First, we plotted depth profiles of water temperature and dissolved oxygen levels and calculated mean water transparency values for each sample period in the spring and fall. For our pelagic insect data, we calculated the mean density, biomass, and individual size of insects collected in the spring and fall. We derived the same metrics between benthic insect samples taken from areas that were frequently, occasionally, or never dewatered. Because of low sample sizes, we provide only a qualitative assessment of these data. Length frequency distributions of fish captured in fyke and gill nets were plotted for each season. For fyke net data, we compared mean catch per unit effort (CPUE) values (by number and biomass) for the two most common fish species collected (northern pikeminnow and redside shiner) and for all fishes combined using a two-sample t-test. Because catch rates were highest in the northern region of the reservoir, we restricted our analyses to this area. Fyke net CPUE values were transformed (log10 + 1) prior to analysis to reduce heterogeneity of variance and account for zero values. Because of relatively low catches in our gill nets, we compared seasonal CPUE for the most common fish species using the nonparametric Mann-Whitney test. Mountain whitefish (*Prosopium williamsoni*) and RBT were excluded from all statistical analyses because of a lack of information on mountain whitefish movements into and out of the reservoir (Petersen and others, 2003) and because RBT were not stocked consistently in all years. Bridgelip suckers (*Catostomus columbianus*) and largescale suckers (*Catostomus macrocheilus*) were combined prior to analysis because juvenile fish were not always identified to species. Finally, population and biomass estimates for the most common fish species were qualitatively compared between seasons.

Fish responses to reservoir dewatering.—We used some of the methods described above to assess the potential effects of consecutive complete dewatering events of Beulah Reservoir that occurred during the summers of 2002, 2003, and 2004. Petersen and Kofoot (2002) and Petersen and others (2003) sampled Beulah Reservoir in 2001 and 2002—prior to dewatering—using methods similar to ours. We considered data from Petersen and Kofoot (2002) and Petersen and others (2003) to be representative of conditions prior to the dewatering events and our data representative of conditions about 1.5 years after the last dewatering. We compared catch data during the spring from each study using methods described above. We also compared changes in the numbers of fish within selected length groups for suckers, northern pikeminnow, and redside shiners between the pre- and post-dewatering catches using a Chi-squared contingency test. For simplicity, we grouped suckers and northern pikeminnow into four size groups (0-99, 100-199, 200-299, and $\geq$ 300 mm) and redside shiners into smaller size groups (0-49, 50-69, 70-89, and $\geq$ 90 mm). Other fish species were not analyzed due to insufficient catches.

Results of Data Analyses

Water Quality and Response to Drawdown

Mean water temperatures at the surface of the reservoir ranged from about 7°C in mid-April to greater than 19°C in early June and from 13°C in mid-October to about 8°C in mid-November (fig. 2). Temperatures near the bottom of the reservoir at the southern (deepest) and middle regions ranged from about 6°C in mid-April to about 12°C in early June. Temperatures peaked at greater than 16°C near the bottom at the northern end of the reservoir during early June. During the fall, temperatures near the bottom of the reservoir ranged from 12°C in mid-October to 8°C in November. Stratification occurred in the southern and middle areas of the reservoir during late April and persisted to at least early June. Stratification was evident only during late April in the northern area of the reservoir. During fall, the reservoir was not stratified but water temperatures decreased gradually with depth. Concentrations of dissolved oxygen in the reservoir were highest during mid-May (9-10.5 mg/L) and generally lowest during mid-October (5-6 mg/L; fig. 3). Mean secchi depths were lowest in the middle of November (0.9 ± 0.07 m; N = 2), highest during early June (1.8 ± 0.08 m; N = 3), and showed little spatial variation.

Reservoir Habitat, Invertebrate Sampling and Response to Drawdown

During 2006, Beulah Reservoir reached a maximum content of about 0.072-km^3 (58,830 acre-ft) on 20 May and declined to a minimum of 0.023-km^3 (18,656 acre-ft) on 14 October (figs. 4 and 5). Refilling of the reservoir began on October 15, just after the start of fall sampling on October 10. From early summer through early fall, the reservoir was drawn down 68 percent, less than typical drawdowns (mean = 86 percent; 1977–2005).

Overall, pelagic invertebrate samples were dominated by Diptera and Hydracarina, with lesser numbers of Coleoptera and Odonata (table 1). Generally, macroinvertebrate densities were highest during May and lowest during November. Chironomid larvae were the most abundant invertebrate collected during spring (mean = 0.97 ± 0.64 individuals/m^3 in May and 0.56 ± 0.97 individuals/m^3 in June). Other invertebrates were rare. In the fall, Hydracarina were the most abundant invertebrate collected (0.40 ± 0.06 individuals/m^3) and no chironomids were collected.

Locations of the reservoir areas that defined the depth strata for our benthic invertebrate samples are shown in figure 6. The benthic insect assemblages consisted primarily of Dipterans (mostly chironomids), Oligochaetes, and Trichopterans (table 2). Benthic invertebrate densities were highest during mid-April and lowest during mid-June. Mean (± SD) densities of Dipterans were considerably lower in areas of the reservoir that were frequently dewatered (143 ± 211 individuals/m^2) compared to areas that were typically inundated (811 ± 249 individuals/m^2 in areas generally not dewatered; 882 ± 561 individuals/m^2 in areas that were occasionally dewatered). Also, Dipterans collected from areas that were frequently dewatered were typically smaller (0.005 ± 0.004 g) than those from other areas (0.015 – 0. 017 ± 0.005 g). Other benthic insect densities were relatively similar between depth strata.

Fish Sampling and Response to Drawdown

Sampling effort for both gear types was expended throughout the reservoir (figs. 7 and 8). In the spring, we collected 10,067 fish representing nine taxa. The most abundant taxa were redside shiners and northern pikeminnow, each comprising 43 percent of our total catch. Other fish collected were bridgelip sucker, largescale sucker, RBT, longnose dace (*Rhinichthys cataractae*), speckled dace (*Rhinichthys osculus*), white crappie (*Pomoxis nigromaculatus*), and sculpins (*Cottus* spp.). The biomass of our catches was dominated by RBT (29 percent), northern pikeminnow (29 percent), and bridgelip and largescale suckers (25 percent). All other fishes comprised the remaining 17 percent of the total biomass. During fall, we collected a total of 5,744 fish representing eight taxa (no speckled dace were collected). Again, the most abundant fish were northern pikeminnow (49 percent) and redside shiners (40 percent) and biomass was dominated by RBT (41 percent), suckers (30 percent), and northern pikeminnow (16 percent). No bull trout were collected in 2006.

Overall, the majority of fish were captured in fyke nets (97-99 percent of all fish caught). Of these fish, 86-95 percent were captured in less than 2 m of water. Only RBT in the spring (70 percent of total catch) and white crappie in the fall (59 percent of total catch) were captured in fyke nets fished deeper than 2 m. Gill net catches were low, with the majority of the fish (81 percent) captured in less than 11 m of water in the spring. No mountain whitefish or RBT were captured in gillnets fished deeper than 11 m. In contrast, the majority of fish collected by gill nets in the fall were captured when nets were fished deeper than 11 m (64 percent). Rainbow trout and largescale suckers were the only species captured more frequently by gill nets in less than 11 m of water during the fall. Overall, 80-85 percent of all fish collected came from the northern half of the reservoir.

In general, the mean sizes of fish of each species were similar between the spring and fall sample periods (table 3 and table 4). One exception to this was white crappies collected in the fall; these fish were up to three times heavier (maximum weight = 128 g) than those collected during the spring (maximum weight = 35 g). Mountain whitefish, RBT, and suckers were the largest fish collected (figs. 9 and 10). We collected a range of sizes of all species, suggesting that several age classes were present and reproduction in the reservoir was successful.

We collected stomach contents from three bull trout that were collected by angling below Agency Valley Dam during the spring of 2006. Dipterans, mostly chironomids, comprised 99 – 100 percent of the diet of these fish.

Mean CPUE by number of Fyke nets for northern pikeminnow, redside shiners, and total fish collected were similar between spring and fall (P > 0.05; table 5). Dace were the only fish for which CPUE decreased substantially after drawdown (spring = 0.25 fish/h; fall = 0.02 fish/h). The catch rates of sculpins (spring = 0.01 fish/h; fall = 0.03 fish/h) and white crappies (spring = 0.06 fish/h; fall = 0.14 fish/h) increased considerably after drawdown. The mean CPUE by biomass of Fyke nets for northern pikeminnow, redside shiners, mountain whitefish, and dace all decreased after drawdown, significantly so only for northern pikeminnow (P < 0.03). In contrast, biomass estimates for sculpins and white crappies increased considerably after drawdown and the biomass of suckers was similar during the two sample periods. Catch rates (by number and biomass) for northern pikeminnow, suckers, and crappies collected with gill nets were significantly higher in the fall than in spring (P < 0.01; table 6), whereas redside shiner CPUE from gill nets was similar between seasons.

The species composition of fish collected with each gear type before and after the 2006 drawdown varied considerably. The relative abundance of fish collected with fyke nets was similar between the pre- and post-drawdown periods but biomass varied considerably (fig. 11). Northern pikeminnow biomass decreased 30 percent and white crappie biomass increased over 20 percent from spring to fall. In addition, sucker biomass increased and redside shiner biomass decreased by less than 20 percent after reservoir drawdown. The most notable changes from our gillnet sampling were an increase in the number of white crappies and a decrease in the biomass of mountain whitefish caught in the fall (fig. 12). The biomass of suckers and northern pikeminnow captured with gill nets was similar to pre-drawdown rates (±2 percent).

Reside shiners and northern pikeminnow were the most abundant fish in Beulah Reservoir during the spring and fall (tables 7 and 8). The fall population estimate for northern pikeminnow < 150 mm (N = 31,772) was less than half that for fish in the spring (N = 78,630). The 95 percent CI's overlapped slightly for estimates from the two sampling periods. Redside shiner population estimates were also considerably lower in the fall (N = 75,842) than in the spring (N = 134,500). However, the 95 percent CI's from these estimates overlapped almost entirely. The population estimates for other species such as suckers (>35,000 in the spring), dace (>14,000 in the spring), RBT (>5,000 in the fall), and sculpins (>950 in the fall) collectively contribute at least 50,000 additional forage fish in Beulah Reservoir. The larger fish of some species (e.g., northern pikeminnow, RBT, and redside shiners) typically composed a small proportion of the population by number, but a considerable proportion by biomass.

Fish Response to Severe Dewatering

Beulah reservoir was completely dewatered to run-of-river levels during the late summer and early fall of 2002, 2003, and 2004 (fig. 13). During these years, dewatering occurred on about August 10 of 2002 and 2003 and on September 18, 2004. The reservoir remained empty (with the exception of some water in the old river channels) until October 12 in 2002, October 16 in 2003, and October 8 in 2004. During the late fall, winter, and early summer of 2002–03, the reservoir filled to a maximum of 0.045 km^3 (36,173 acre-ft). During the same period in 2003–04, the reservoir filled to 0.064 km^3 (52,104 acre-ft; table 9).

The catch rates (by number) of northern pikeminnow and suckers using gill nets were significantly lower in the spring of 2006 than in the two years prior to dewatering (table 6). The biomass of these species also was significantly lower in 2006 than in 2001 and 2002 ($P < 0.001$). The catch rates of white crappie (by number and biomass) differed slightly between the pre- and post-dewatering periods, but differences were not significant. The catch rates (by number and biomass) of redside shiners and mountain whitefish in 2006 ranged from 152 – 271 percent of the values in 2001 and 2002, but the results did not differ significantly.

The percent composition of fish taxa in the reservoir in 2001 and 2002 prior to dewatering was similar to that in 2006 (tables 10 and 11). Notable exceptions included reductions in the abundance and biomass of suckers, the biomass of northern pikeminnow, and increases in the numbers and biomass of mountain whitefish in 2006 when compared to 2001 and 2002. The biomass of redside shiners was higher in 2006 relative to the pre-dewatering years despite a reduction in their percent composition. Compared to samples from 2001 and 2002, the percent composition of northern pikeminnow decreased and suckers increased in 2006. The percent composition of other species was similar between samples collected in the different years.

The size structure of some fish species differed between catches in 2001 and 2002 and catches in 2006 (fig. 14). In 2001 and 2002, before dewatering, 41 percent of northern pikeminnow and 79 percent of suckers were larger than 100 mm and 79 percent of redside shiners were larger than 50 mm. In 2006, only 8 percent of northern pikeminnow and 32 percent of suckers were larger than 100 mm and 53 percent of redside shiners were larger than 50 mm. In 2006, northern pikeminnow and suckers larger than 200 mm represented <4 percent of the total catch compared to 15 percent and 67 percent before dewatering. In 2006, the majority of fish collected were smaller than those collected in the years prior to reservoir dewatering and were likely young-of-year fishes. Differences in size composition of fish collected before and after dewatering were significant (P < 0.001) for northern pikeminnow, suckers, and redside shiners.

Implications of Findings to Potential Forage for Bull Trout

The purpose of our research on Beulah Reservoir was twofold. First, we wanted to document the abundance, biomass, and general distribution of potential forage items (fish and invertebrates) for bull trout. Second, we wanted to determine whether typical reservoir operations (i.e., summer drawdown) adversely affect the prey base for bull trout. Eventually, all of this information should help establish minimum pool levels in Beulah Reservoir for the maintenance of forage fish and bull trout. Our results indicate that a large amount of potential forage for bull trout exists in the reservoir, at least during the times that we sampled. The drawdown in the summer of 2006 was not extreme. As such, we detected few significant changes in the fish community when catches in the spring were compared to those in the fall. We did note, however, that insect populations in areas that are frequently dewatered were lower than those in areas that remain inundated, which could have implications for bull trout foraging at certain times of the year. Finally, we noted a variety of differences in the abundance, biomass, and size composition of the fish community during the pre-dewatering years compared to those found in our post-dewatering sampling in 2006. Overall, however, the fish and insect community in Beulah Reservoir in 2006 did not seem significantly impaired by the complete dewatering that took place in 2002, 2003, and 2004.

During our sampling in 2006, we collected more than 15,000 fish , which represented all the resident fish species (with the exception of chiselmouth *Acrocheilus alutaceus* and bull trout) that historically inhabited the Malheur drainage (Malheur Watershed Counsel and Burns Piute Tribe, 2004). Although we collected fish throughout the reservoir, most were captured in the shallow northern areas and seemed concentrated near areas of cover such as willows (*Salix* spp.) During spring, fish were uncommon in the deepest areas of the reservoir, indicating that they preferred warmer and shallower shoreline areas. In contrast, during the fall, fish were more numerous in deep areas of the reservoir, suggesting that some species or age classes of fish use deep water during the summer and early fall to avoid thermal stress or for additional forage opportunities. The dewatering events of 2002–04 were in part targeted at eradicating the white crappie population in the reservoir. Our results suggest that these attempts were unsuccessful, because our catches were similar to those reported prior to reservoir dewatering (Petersen and others, 2003). Perhaps because of the moderate summer drawdown of 2006, white crappies were larger than those captured previously (Petersen and others, 2003). In the fall, white crappies in Beulah Reservoir reached sizes at which their diet may have shifted from zooplankton and insects to primarily fish (Ellison, 1984), potentially increasing competition with bull trout for prey.

During the spring and fall, macroinvertebrate numbers in Beulah Reservoir were low, except for Dipterans (primarily planktonic chironomid larvae) during the spring. Our invertebrate sampling was not extensive, however, did not include reservoir-wide benthic or surface estimates of insect densities, and was meant to identify macroinvertebrates that were highly abundant, not to thoroughly describe the insect community. Although information on the diets of bull trout in Beulah Reservoir is not available, other studies suggest that much of their diet consists of invertebrates during cold water periods in lakes and reservoirs. For example, Wilhelm and others (1999) noted that the diet of bull trout (> 250 mm) in high alpine lakes of the Canadian Rocky Mountains (where other fishes were not present) contained more than 90 percent chironomids following ice out. Beauchamp and Van Tassel (2001) reported that 69-88 percent of the diet of bull trout (200-400 mm) consisted of invertebrates from January-May in Lake Billy Chinook, Oregon. Finally, diet information from several bull trout collected in the NFMR just below Agency Valley Dam by personnel from the Burns Paiute Tribe during the spring of 2006 indicated a diet of mostly chironomids. Collectively, this information suggests that chironomids are an important forage item for bull trout in many areas at certain times of the year and should be considered in our forage investigations at Beulah Reservoir.

Most of the potential fish forage for bull trout in Beulah Reservoir includes redside shiners and smaller size classes of northern pikeminnow. Other fish, such as dace, sculpins, small rainbow trout, and suckers, could also contribute to the diet of bull trout, but these fish were less abundant. During the spring, populations of redside shiners and northern pikeminnow were higher than those in the fall. There are many possible explanations for this, including an influx of subyearling fishes from the NFMR and Warm Spring Creek during late fall and early winter, changes in gear vulnerability, losses due to predation, outmigration of larger fishes, and direct losses associated with the summer drawdown. Although abundance estimates were lower during the fall, fish biomass may continue to increase throughout the fall, winter, and spring periods if over-winter growth occurs. For example, average extrapolated weights for redside shiners (2.0 g) and northern pikeminnow (7.6 g) during the spring were about twice that estimated for the fall period (0.8, 3.9 g). This suggests that forage biomass could double over the winter based on fish growth alone. In addition, all fishes that were too small to capture during the fall likely contribute additional biomass as growth occurs during the winter.

Fish population and biomass estimates were limited by our ability to recapture fish. Therefore, we estimated population sizes and biomass only for the most abundant species that we consistently recaptured. These included redside shiners, northern pikeminnow, suckers, and dace during the spring, and redside shiners, northern pikeminnow, RBT, and sculpins in the fall. Our population and biomass estimates should be viewed with caution for several reasons. First, some of the shoreline area in the reservoir could not be effectively sampled with fyke nets due to shallow water depths and problems associated with fences near the shore. Based on visual observations, these relatively shallow areas contained reasonable numbers of fish that were not accounted for in our population estimates unless they moved into areas that we did sample. Second, many fish may have remained offshore during most of our sampling and were not vulnerable to the gill nets we used. Finally, the population estimates for many species and size classes in the fall had high variances due to reduced sampling effort and inconsistent recapture rates for less common species. These caveats should be consistent between sample periods, however, and our estimates provide some insight into the effects of reservoir operations on forage availability, allow for comparisons between different water years, and should be useful for future bioenergetic analyses.

The summer drawdowns in Beulah Reservoir do have measurable effects on the insect and fish communities. The drawdown of 2006 was not considered extreme and, in fact, was relatively mild compared to those in previous years. Nevertheless, we noted some distinct changes in shoreline chironomid populations and characteristics of our fish catches between spring and fall. We found fewer and smaller chironomids in substrates of Beulah Reservoir that were typically dewatered compared to areas that remained inundated. Such a finding is similar to that in other studies assessing the effects of reservoir drawdown on the size and numbers of chironomids (Furey and others, 2006). Sampling invertebrates was not a central focus of our study and, because insects may be important to the diet of bull trout in Beulah Reservoir, they warrant further consideration.

Despite the reduction of near shore habitat available for fish in the fall, our catches of fish in fyke nets were similar between the spring and fall, indicating that fish densities did not change appreciably. Although numbers of fish in the spring and fall were generally similar, total biomass decreased in the fall. This was likely due to increased catches of smaller sized fish during the fall and the offshore distribution of age-1 or older northern pikeminnow. Gill net catches of northern pikeminnow, suckers, and white crappie increased in the fall, suggesting an increased density of these fishes in offshore areas. It seems likely that the lower pool volume concentrates fish in the offshore areas, leading to higher catch rates. Mountain whitefish numbers decreased in the fall, suggesting that these fish may have left the reservoir in the summer and had not returned prior to our sampling. Finally, in the fall, catches of redside shiners had an increased number of smaller fish and catches of suckers contained larger fish than we saw in the spring. Overall, a comparison of data collected in the spring and fall shows that the drawdown of 2006 did not drastically harm the forage fish community in Beulah Reservoir. We reiterate, however, that the drawdown of 2006 was relatively moderate. To fully understand the effects of summer drawdown on the aquatic community of Beulah Reservoir would require multiple, consecutive years of study under a variety of environmental and reservoir management scenarios.

Evaluating the effects of the complete dewatering of Beulah Reservoir in 2002, 2003, and 2004 is tenuous because of variations in gear, protocols, environmental conditions, and the time that has passed between studies. However, our analysis suggests several things. First, the reduced gill net catches of larger northern pikeminnow and suckers in 2006 were probably influenced by the previous dewatering events. During dewatering, many large fish likely would have emigrated or exhibited higher mortality rates than in normal water years, leaving fewer to catch in subsequent years. In contrast, the catch rates of redside shiners were similar between the pre- and post-dewatering sampling periods, suggesting that these fish were relatively resilient to dewatering. These fish may have a superior ability to survive in the remaining water and have higher reproductive success and juvenile recruitment in a relatively predator-free post-dewatering environment. We noted that fish taxa were similar between pre- and post-dewatering periods. This suggests that all taxa were able to withstand stresses associated with dewatering or that individuals were able to re-colonize the reservoir once it was refilled. Perhaps the most obvious effects of reservoir dewatering were changes in the size composition of suckers and northern pikeminnow. Prior to dewatering, a variety of sucker and northern pikeminnow size classes representing diverse age structures were collected. During 2006 sampling, most individuals of these taxa were smaller subyearling and yearling sized fishes, based on length frequency data. As mentioned earlier, larger individuals may have emigrated or were subsequently killed during dewatering, but those that remained achieved high reproductive success and juvenile recruitment. The size distributions of redside shiners were slightly different between the pre- and post-dewatering periods. The significantly larger catches of redside shiners in 2006, though slightly lower than before dewatering, indicate higher survival during dewatering or faster growth rates than those reported in the literature (Houston and Belk, 2006). Paller (1997) documented similar increases in smaller individuals and decreases in larger individuals following a four year drawdown of Par Pond, South Carolina, for warm water fish species.

We did not capture any bull trout during our sampling in 2006, despite sampling in water conditions were suitable for bull trout (i.e. <15°C; Rieman and McIntrye, 1993) and during times when they could have been in the reservoir (Gonzalez, 1998; Schwab and others, 1999). The collection (by angling) of a few bull trout below Agency Valley Dam by the Burns Piute Tribe in 2006 indicates that fish were in the reservoir sometime during the late fall, winter, and spring of 2005-06, but we did not catch any. In the future, we hope to try alternative sampling techniques such as trammel nets, angling, or large fish traps, and target areas of the reservoir where other researchers have been successful capturing bull trout in the past.

Proposed Future Research

We plan to sample the aquatic community in Beulah Reservoir during spring 2007, shortly after ice out, and in the fall. The information collected in 2007 will complement that from 2006 and allow for more informed decisions regarding future reservoir management. We are currently completing a bioenergetics model parameterized specifically for bull trout. We will use the model, along with information on temperature and energy density of prey, to predict the forage base necessary to sustain bull trout residing in Beulah Reservoir for various lengths of time. These analyses, along with our field information, will allow development of conservation pool limits for Beulah Reservoir, which will benefit bull trout. Continued long-term monitoring of the forage populations will provide greater understanding of the effects of water management and assist with the development of conservation pool levels.

Acknowledgments

We thank Alexis Koenings for her invaluable assistance in the field and during data processing. Timothy Walters and Raymond Perkins from Oregon Department of Fish and Wildlife and Lawrence Schwabe and Jason Fenton of the Department of Fish and Wildlife of the Burns Paiute Tribe provided field gear and technical advice. This manuscript benefited from the careful peer review of Craig Haskell and Rusty Rodriguez and was funded by the Bureau of Reclamation. Reference to trade, firm, or corporation names does not imply endorsement by the U.S. Department of Interior or U.S. Geological Survey.

References Cited

Bauchamp, D.A., and Van Tassel, J.J., 2001, Modeling seasonal trophic interactions of adfluvial bull trout in Lake Billy Chinook, Oregon: Transactions of the American Fisheries Society, v. 130, p. 204-216.

Bayley, P.B., and Osborne, L.L., 1993, Natural rehabilitation of stream fish populations in an Illinois catchment: Freshwater Biology, v. 29, p. 295-300.

Benson, N.G., and Hudson, P.L., 1975, Effects of a reduced fall drawdown on benthos abundance in Lake Francis Case: Transactions of the American Fisheries Society, v. 104, p. 526-528.

Bureau of Reclamation, 2002, Beulah Reservoir water quality modeling study: Denver, Colorado, Vale Irrigation Project, Oregon.

Ellison, D.G., 1984, Trophic dynamics of a Nebraska Black Crappie and White Crappie Population: North American Journal of Fisheries Management, v. 4, p. 355-364.

Estes, R.D., 1972, Ecological impact of fluctuating water levels in reservoirs; Ecological impact of water resource development; Water, man, and nature symposium: Washington, D.C., U.S. Bureau of Reclamation, Report RECERC-72-17.

Fraley, J.J., and Shepard, B.B., 1989, Life history and population status of migratory bull trout (Salvelinus confluentus) in the Flathead Lake and River System, Montana: Northwest Science, v. 63, no. 4, p. 133-143.

Furey, P.C., Nordin, R.N., and Mazumber, A., 2006, Littoral benthic macroinvertabrates under contrasting drawdown in a reservoir and a lake: Journal of the North American Benthological Society, v. 25, no. 1, p. 19-31.

Gaboury, M.N., and Patalas, J.W., 1984, Influence of water-level drawdown on the fish populations of Cross Lake, Manitoba: Canadian Journal of Fisheries and Aquatic Sciences, v. 41, p. 118-125.

Gonzalez, D., 1998, Evaluate the life history of salmonids in the Malheur River Basin: Portland, Oregon, Annual Report to the Bonneville Power Administration.

Graham, P., Penkal, R., McMullin, S., Schladweiler, P., Mayes, H., Riggs, V., and Klaver, R.W., 1981, Montana: Recommendations for fish and wildlife program: Portland, Oregon, prepared for Pacific Northwest Electric Council.

Houston, D.D., and Belk, M.C., 2006, Geographic variation in somatic growth of Redside Shiner: Transactions of the American Fisheries Society, v. 135, p. 801-810.

Lagler, K.F, 1956, Freshwater Fishery Biology: Dubuque, Iowa, W.M.C. Brown.

Lantz, K.E., Davis, J.T., Hughes, J.S., and Schafer, H.E. Jr., 1967, Water level fluctuation—its effects on vegetation control and fish population management: Proceedings of the Annual Conference Southeastern Association of Game and Fish Commissioners, v. 18, p. 483-494.

Malheur Watershed Council and Burns Paiute Tribe, 2004, Malheur River Subbasin Assessment and Management Plan For Fish and Wildlife Mitigation, Appendix A, Part 2 – Assessment Aquatic: Portland, Oregon, Northwest Power and Conservation Council.

Matthews, W.J., 1986, Fish Faunal structure in an Ozark stream: stability, persistence and a catastrophic flood: Copeia, v. 1986, no. 2, p. 388-397.

Muhlfeld, C.C., Glutting, S., Hunt, R., Daniels, D., and Marotz, B., 2003, Winter diel habitat use and movement by subadult bull trout in the Upper Flathead River, Montana: North American Journal of Fisheries Management, v. 23, p. 163-171.

Nichols, S.A., 1975, The impact of over winter drawdown on the aquatic vegetation of the Chippewa flowage, Wisconsin, USA: Transactions of the Wisconsin Academy of Sciences, Arts, and Letters, v. 63, p. 176-186.

Paller, M.H., 1997, Recovery of a reservoir fish community from drawdown related impacts: North American Journal of Fisheries Management, v. 17, p. 726-733.

Petersen, J.H., and Kofoot E.E., 2002, Conditions for growth and survival of bull trout in Beulah Reservoir, Oregon: Boise, Idaho, 2001 Annual Report to the Bureau of Reclamation, Pacific Northwest Region.

Petersen, J.H., Kofoot, E.E., and Rose, B., 2003, Conditions for growth and survival of bull trout in Beulah Reservoir, Oregon: Boise, Idaho, U.S. Geological Survey, 2002 Annual Report to the Bureau of Reclamation, Pacific Northwest Region, 44 p.

Ratliff, D.E., and Howell, P.J., 1992, The status of bull trout populations in Oregon, *in* Howell, P.J., and Buchanan, D.V., eds., Proceedings of the Gearhart Mountain bull trout workshop: Corvallis, Oregon, Oregon Chapter of the American Fisheries Society, p. 10-17.

Rieman, B.E., and Mcintyre, J.D., 1993, Demographic and habitat requirements for conservation of bull trout: Ogden, Utah, U.S. Forest Service, General Technical Report INT-302, 38 p.

Schneider, J.C., 1998, Lake fish population estimates by mark-and-recapture methods, chapter 8, *in* J.C. Schneider, ed., Manual of fisheries survey methods II: with periodic updates: Ann Arbor, Michigan, Michigan Department of Natural Resources, Fisheries Special Report 25.

Schwabe, L., and Tiley, M., 1999, Evaluation of the life history of native salmonids in the Malheur River Basin: Portland, Oregon, Annual Report to the Bonneville Power Administration Project 9701900/9701901.

Wilhelm, F.M., Parker, B.R., Schindlerm, D.W., and Donald, D.B., 1999, Seasonal food habits of bull trout from a small alpine lake in the Canadian Rocky Mountains: Transactions of the American Fisheries Society, v. 128, p. 1176-1192.

Woods, P.F., and Falter, C.M., 1982, Limnological investigations: Lake Koocanusa, Montana, Part 4 – Factors controlling primary productivity: Seattle, Washington, U.S. Army Corps of Engineers, Seattle District, Special Report 82-15.

Table 1. Number (N), standard deviation (SD), and biomass of planktonic macroinvertebrates per m³ collected in Beulah Reservoir in 2006. Composite samples of three tows with a plankton net were collected in each of four regions of the reservoir (NW, SW, NE, and SE). Estimates within each zone were averaged to estimate reservoir densities.

Period	Diptera				Hydracarina				Odonata				Coleoptera			
Date	N	SD	Bio-mass (g)	SD	N	SD	Bio-mass (g)	SD	N	SD	Bio-mass (g)	SD	N	SD	Bio-mass (g)	SD
Spring																
5/14/2006	0.97	0.64	0.008	0.006	0.12	0.15	0ᵃ	0ᵃ	0	-	0	-	0	-	0	-
6/10/2006	0.56	0.97	0.002	0.004	0.16	0.19	0ᵃ	0ᵃ	0	-	0	-	0	-	0	-
Fall																
10/14/2006	0	-	0	-	0.16	0.11	0ᵃ	0ᵃ	0.06	0.08	0.001	.0001	0	-	0	-
10/27/2006	0	-	0	-	0.40	0.06	0ᵃ	0ᵃ	0	0	0	0	0.03	0.06	0ᵃ	0ᵃ
11/10/2006	0	-	0	-	0	-	0	-	0	0	0	0	0	-	0	-

ᵃValues equaled zero with rounding error

15

Table 2. Number (per m^2), standard deviation (SD), and biomass (g/m^2) of aquatic macroinvertebrates collected in Beulah Reservoir during 2006. Locations were generally not dewatered, occasionally dewatered, and frequently dewatered. Values represent the mean of two grab samples unless noted.

Location Date	Diptera				Oligochaeta				Trichoptera			
	N	SD	Biomass	SD	N	SD	Biomass	SD	N	SD	Biomass	SD
Not Dewatered												
17 April[a]	1,076	-	19.5	-	904	-	4.0	-	0	-	0	-
30 April	775	548	9.4	0.7	516	183	1.7	1.12	0	0	0	0
10 June	581	213	12.7	2.7	21	22	0.2	0.3	0	0	0	0
Occasionally Dewatered												
17 April[a]	1,162	-	14.1	-	258	-	0.7	-	0	-	0	-
30 April	1,248	365	13.7	2.8	22	30	0.1	0.1	43	0	0.3	0.1
10 June	236	30	5.0	0.3	0	0	0	0	0	0	0	0
Frequently Dewatered												
17 April	21	30	0.1	0.2	646	852	2.3	3.2	0	0	0	0
30 April	21	30	0.2	0.3	129	122	0.9	0.6	0	0	0	0
10 June	387	426	0.5	0.2	129	61	0.9	0.6	43	61	1.0	1.5

[a]Only one sample collected due to weather

Table 3. Mean, minimum (min), maximum (max), standard deviation (SD), and sample size (N) of fish measured and weighed in Beulah Reservoir during spring, 2006. Mean length and weight values were corrected for fish whose lengths and weights were extrapolated from regressions. Corrected values were excluded from SD calculations.

Species	Length (mm)				Weight (g)				
	Mean	Min	Max	SD	Mean	Min	Max	SD	N
Bridgelip sucker	165	53	440	92.7	132.5	1.7	1,210.0	276.7	77
Largescale sucker	105	40	448	46.9	27.4	1.5	1,125.0	96.9	432
Unidentified sucker	84	36	488	55.1	25.3	0.7	1,960.0	176.3	275
Northern pikeminnow	71	28	410	33.5	7.6	0.3	1,105.0	51.2	4382
Redside shiner	51	22	111	11.6	2.0	0.2	19.6	2.8	4450
Longnose dace	47	32	72	7.2	1.3	0.4	4.5	0.9	365
Speckled dace	49	35	64	6.7	1.2	0.9	3.0	0.68	41
Redband trout	175	67	563	132.8	206.4	3.7	1,850.0	429.7	165
White crappie	99	68	129	13.0	17.0	4.4	35.1	6.9	75
Sculpin spp.	70	50	90	11.6	5.5	1.6	10.6	3.2	22
Mountain whitefish	271	163	340	55.2	293.0	42.4	590.0	160.9	27
Bull trout	296	284	311	13.9	297	275.0	342.0	38.7	3

17

Table 4. Mean, minimum (min), maximum (max), standard deviation (SD), and sample size (N) of fish measured and weighed in Beulah Reservoir during fall, 2006. Mean length and weight values were corrected for fish whose lengths and weights were extrapolated from regressions. Corrected values were excluded from SD calculations.

Taxa	Length (mm)				Weight (g)				
	Mean	Min	Max	SD	Mean	Min	Max	SD	N
Bridgelip sucker	122	40	280	80.7	56.3	2.6	166.1	89.1	48
Largescale sucker	138	43	395	88.7	78.1	1.1	875.0	172.6	236
Northern pikeminnow	54	22	325	32.6	3.9	0.2	420.5	50.4	2,789
Redside shiner	39	22	106	14.2	0.8	0.1	9.8	2.0	2,288
Longnose dace	45	34	67	7.2	1.1	-	-	-	18
Redband trout	173	64	502	131.3	192.7	2.4	1,505	337.3	152
White crappie	127	83	198	31.8	42.0	8.7	128.1	44.1	159
Sculpin spp.	65	40	102	15.5	4.7	2.8	6.8	1.8	53
Mountain whitefish	139	-	-	-	26.9	-	-	-	1

Table 5. The level of effort expended during Fyke net sampling in Beulah Reservoir in 2006 and the mean, standard deviation (SD), and maximum catch per hour (CPH; by number and biomass) of fish collected with small mesh Fyke nets before and after the drawdown of 2006. Minimum CPH for all taxa and time periods was zero.

	Pre-drawdown (spring 2006)		Post drawdown (fall 2006)	
	Fyke net effort			
N of sets	71		39	
Total hours	1,650		1,143	
Mean soak (h)	23		29	
	N	Biomass (g)	N	Biomass (g)
Northern pikeminnow				
Mean	2.68	15.28	2.90	4.28
SD	4.33	27.01	6.73	7.85
Maximum	20.41	150.92	36.95	30.06
Redside shiner				
Mean	2.91	5.52	2.68	2.14
SD	6.61	13.29	6.08	4.82
Maximum	44.31	89.73	27.51	24.15
Sucker spp.				
Mean	0.32	7.73	0.27	7.62
SD	0.84	19.97	0.34	10.82
Maximum	4.97	116.89	1.8	40.46
Mountain whitefish				
Mean	0.00	0.73	0.00	0.03
SD	0.01	4.35	0.01	0.18
Maximum	0.09	28.43	0.04	0.18
Dace				
Mean	0.25	0.35	0.02	0.02
SD	0.56	0.72	0.05	0.06
Maximum	2.82	3.58	0.18	0.30
Sculpin spp.				
Mean	0.01	0.07	0.06	0.28
SD	0.03	0.16	0.15	0.65
Maximum	0.15	0.70	0.81	3.33
White crappie				
Mean	0.03	0.44	0.14	6.91
SD	0.07	1.09	0.23	10.99
Maximum	0.37	5.82	1.03	44.86

Table 6. mean, standard deviation (SD), and maximum catch per hour (CPH; by number and biomass) of fish collected with gill nets before the summer dewatering of the reservoir during 2002 – 2004 (Petersen and Kofoot 2003) and before and after the drawdown of 2006. Bold values indicate significant (P < 0.05) differences in CPH between the springs of 2001 – 2002 and 2006. Italicized values indicate significant differences between the spring and fall of 2006. Minimum CPH for all taxa and time periods was zero.

	Pre-dewatering (spring 2001-2002)		Post-dewatering; Pre-drawdown (spring 2006)		Post drawdown (fall 2006)	
	Gill-netting effort					
N of sets	66		142		47	
Total hours	88.5		61.3		16.6	
Mean soak time (h)	1.34		0.43		0.35	
	N	Biomass (g)	N	Biomass (g)	N	Biomass (g)
Northern pikeminnow						
Mean	**1.27**	**254.6**	*0.99*	*84.4*	*6.09*	*327.5*
SD	2.40	430.7	2.60	217.6	9.20	548.0
Maximum	13.71	2,492.6	17.50	1,264.2	38.82	2,691.2
Redside shiner						
Mean	0.07	0.6	0.19	1.6	0.19	1.3
SD	0.26	2.2	0.78	6.7	0.73	5.1
Maximum	1.30	11.0	4.61	38.3	3.53	24.0
Suckers						
Mean	**0.92**	**311.2**	*0.20*	*100.2*	*1.78*	*373.4*
SD	1.56	595.4	0.78	413.7	2.48	5480.0
Maximum	10.8	4,046.4	5.46	2,904.0	9.00	2,322.2
Mountain whitefish						
Mean	0.20	61.4	0.35	93.3	0	0
SD	0.54	165.0	1.00	299.9	0	0
Maximum	2.95	852.8	6.32	1,689.5	0	0
White crappie						
Mean	0.03	3.01	*0.01*	*0.2*	*1.49*	*31.6*
SD	0.23	22.13	0.16	1.8	3.39	68.8
Maximum	2.00	197	1.9	21.9	17.65	284.9

Table 7. Population size, 95% confidence intervals, and biomass estimates of selected fish taxa and size cohorts in Beulah Reservoir during the spring, 2006. Biomass estimates were derived from the mean weight for each cohort.

Species Cohort	Population (N)	95% Population CI (N)	Biomass Estimate (kg)	95% Biomass CI (kg)
Spring 2006				
Northern pikeminnow				
<101 mm	70,400	101,284-39,515	153.4	220.7-86.1
101-160 mm	8,230	12,161-4,299	234.1	345.9-122.3
161-200 mm	3,885	15,236-(7,466)	234.2	918.6-(450.2)
>200 mm	865	1,835-(105)	177.8	377.2-(21.6)
Total	83,379	116,194-50,563	799.5	1862-(263)
Redside shiner				
<68 mm	124,906	168,973-80,839	190.9	258.2-123.5
≥68 mm	9,594	15,784-3,404	62.7	103.2-22.2
Total	134,500	178,438-90,560	253.6	361.4-145.8
Sucker spp.				
<76 mm	15,233	33,086-(2,620)	38.3	83.1-(6.6)
76-150 mm	20,333	30,837-9,830	51.1	77.5-24.7
151-200 mm[a]	1,644	3,133-155	106.8	203.5-10.1
>150 mm	5,017	9,109-925	1,841.9	3,344.0-339.7
Total	40,583	61,485-19,682	1,931.2	3,504.6-357.8
Dace spp.				
Total	14,053	23,217-4,889	17.9	29.5-6.2

[a]Values not included in total population estimate

Table 8. Population size, 95% confidence intervals, and biomass estimates of selected fish species and size cohorts in Beulah Reservoir during the fall, 2006. Biomass estimates were derived from the mean weight for each cohort.

Species Cohort	Population (N)	95% Population CI (N)	Biomass Estimate (kg)	95% Biomass CI (kg)
Fall 2006				
Northern pikeminnow				
< 101 mm	29,848	45,463-14,232	44.4	67.7-21.2
< 150 mm	31,772	46,513-17,030	74.5	109.1-39.9
Redside shiner				
< 68 mm	71,115	164,147-(21,917)	56.9	131.3-(17.5)
≥ 68 mm	4,727	6,507-2,947	27.7	38.2-17.3
Total	75,842	167,158-(15,473)	84.6	169.5-(0.2)
Sculpin spp.				
Total	960	1,596-323	4.3	7.1-1.4
Redband rainbow trout				
<101	2,499	5,649-(651)	15.5	35.0-(4.0)
<151	5,147	14,506-(4,211)	52.2	147.1-(42.7)

Table 9. Minimum, maximum, mean, and standard deviation of water volume (in acre-feet) in Beulah Reservoir from 2000 – 2006 calculated from BOR gage data. Years in bold indicate that fish and other sampling occurred that year. Annual drawdown shows the percent of drawdown calculated from the yearly maximum volume.

Reservoir volume	2000	**2001**	**2002**	2003	2004	2005	**2006**
			Water year				
Minimum	10,582	1,725	0	0	0	8,321	18,656
Maximum	59,680	40,411	47,012	36,173	52,105	59,118	58,830
Mean	33,409	17,775	16,195	13,426	19,878	26,650	36,277
SD	17,336	13,087	15,015	12,040	17,627	16,798	13,972
Annual Drawdown (%)	82	96	100	100	100	86	68

Table 10. Percent composition (by number) of fish species collected during the springs of 2001 and 2002 (before the dewatering events of 2002, 2003, and 2004), and during the spring and fall of 2006 (before and after the drawdown of 2006).

Gear type and species	Pre dewatering (spring 2001-2002)	Post dewatering; pre-drawdown (spring 2006)	Post drawdown (fall 2006)
Percent collected by number			
Gill Net			
White crappie	0.8	1.0	15.7
Northern pikeminnow	56.6	55.9	63.4
Redside shiner	3.0	11.8	1.7
Sucker spp.	34.2	10.8	19.2
Mountain whitefish	5.5	20.6	0
Fyke Net			
Sculpin spp.	0	0.2	1.6
White crappie	0.7	0.4	3.9
Northern pikeminnow	40.3	42.8	49.0
Redside shiner	53.1	44.9	37.6
Sucker spp.	5.9	7.5	1.6
Mountain whitefish	0	0.0	0.0
Dace	0	4.2	0.5

Table 11. Percent composition (by biomass) of fish species collected during the springs of 2001 and 2002 (before the dewatering events of 2002, 2003, and 2004) and during the spring and fall of 2006 (before and after the drawdown of 2006).

Gear type and species	Pre dewatering (spring 2001-2002)	Post dewatering; pre-drawdown (spring 2006)	Post drawdown (fall 2006)
	Percent collected by biomass		
	Gill Net		
White crappie	0	0.1	4.2
Northern pikeminnow	31.9	32.6	45.4
Redside shiner	0.1	0.6	0.1
Sucker spp.	59.6	36.5	50.3
Mountain whitefish	8.3	30.3	0
	Fyke Net		
Sculpin	0	0.2	1.0
White crappie	0.5	1.4	24.7
Northern pikeminnow	62.3	43.7	14.2
Redside shiner	3.8	17.0	6.3
Sucker spp.	33.4	34.2	53.7
Mountain whitefish	0	2.5	0.1
Dace	0	1.1	0.1

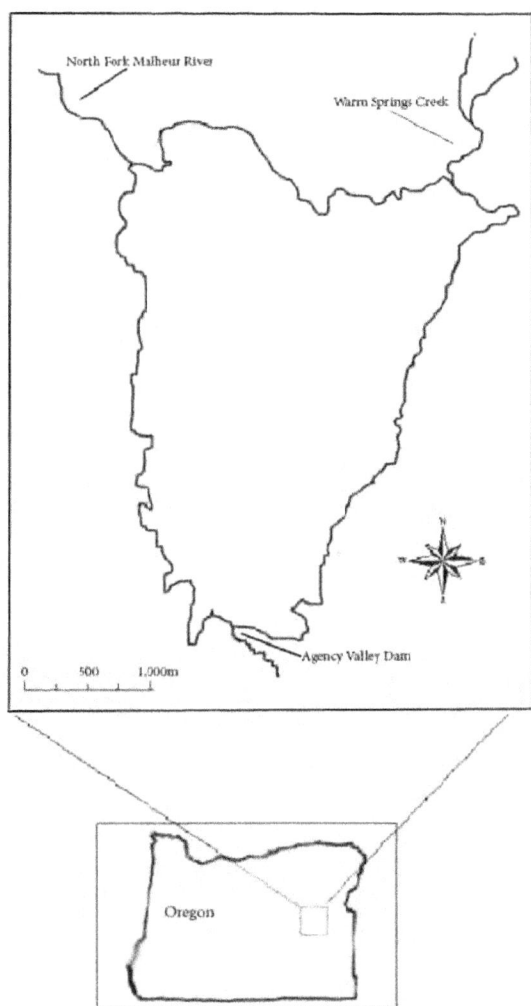

Figure 1. Location and tributaries of Beulah Reservoir, Oregon. The North Fork of the Malheur River enters from the northwest and exits to the south. Warm Spring Creek enters from the northeast.

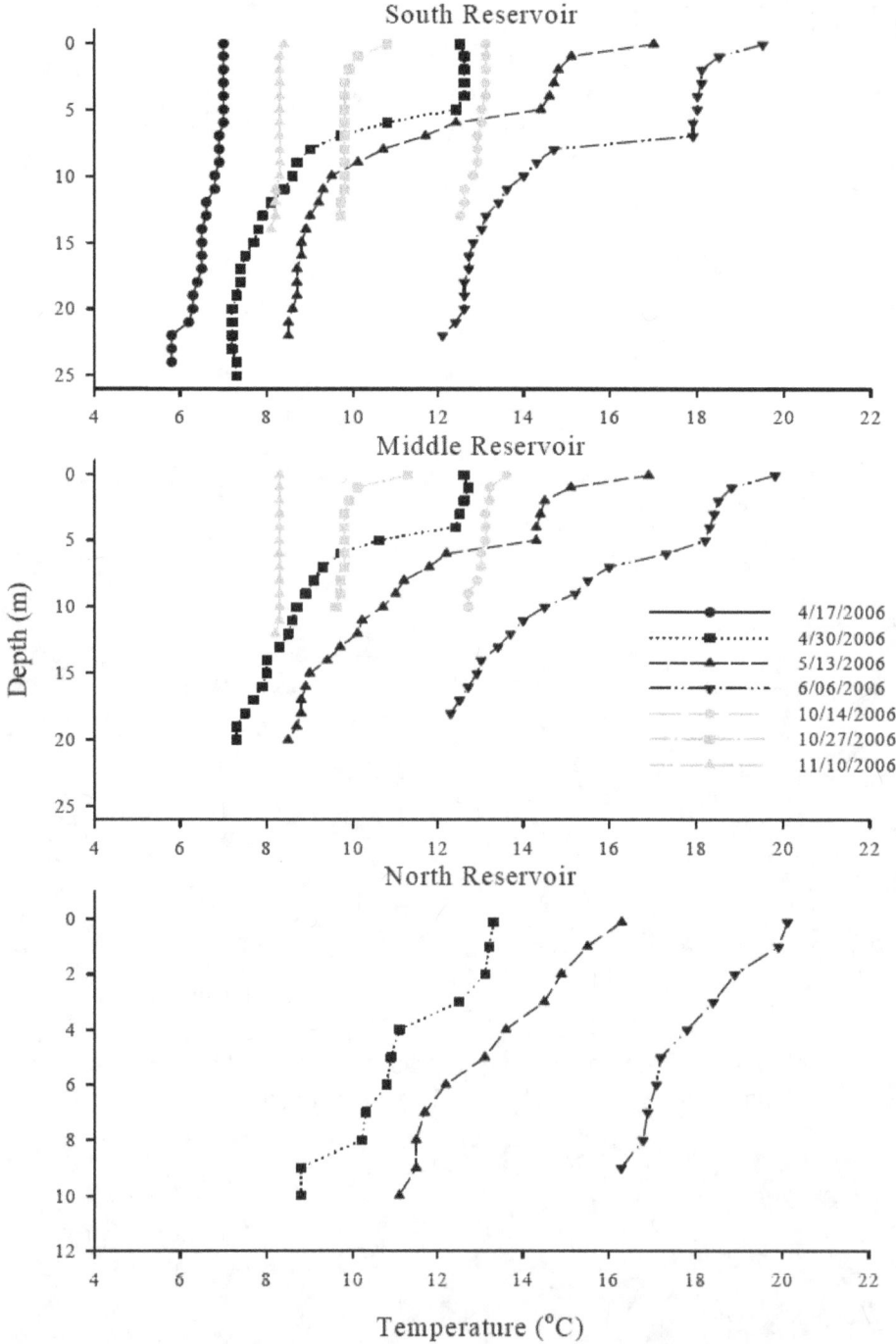

Figure 2. Temperature profiles at three sites in Beulah Reservoir. Sites were sampled during the spring and early summer (black symbols) and in the fall (gray symbols). The north part of the reservoir was not sampled during the fall.

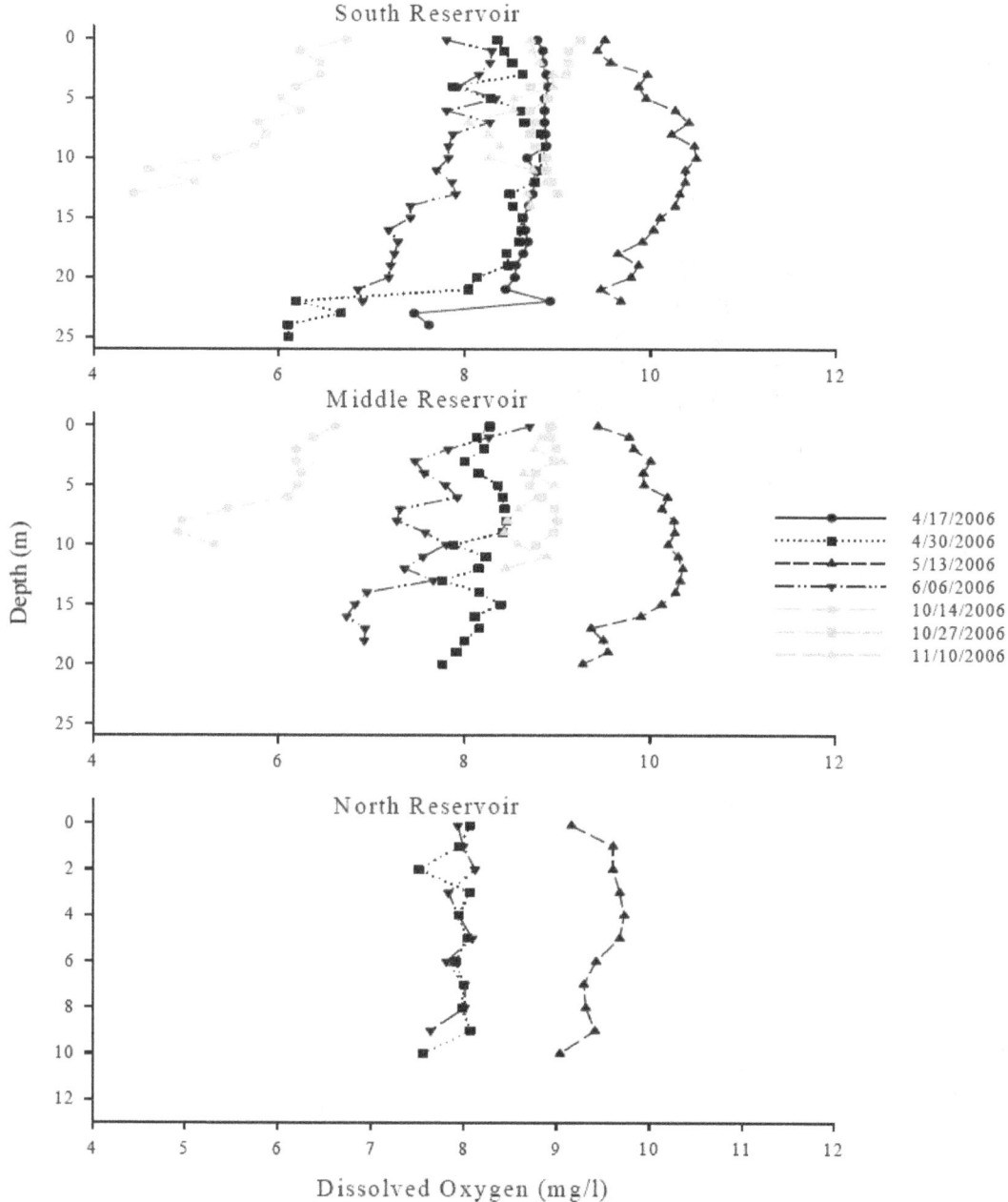

Figure 3. Dissolved oxygen profiles at three general locations in Beulah Reservoir. Sites were sampled during the spring and early summer (black symbols) and in the fall (gray symbols). The north part of the reservoir was not sampled during the fall.

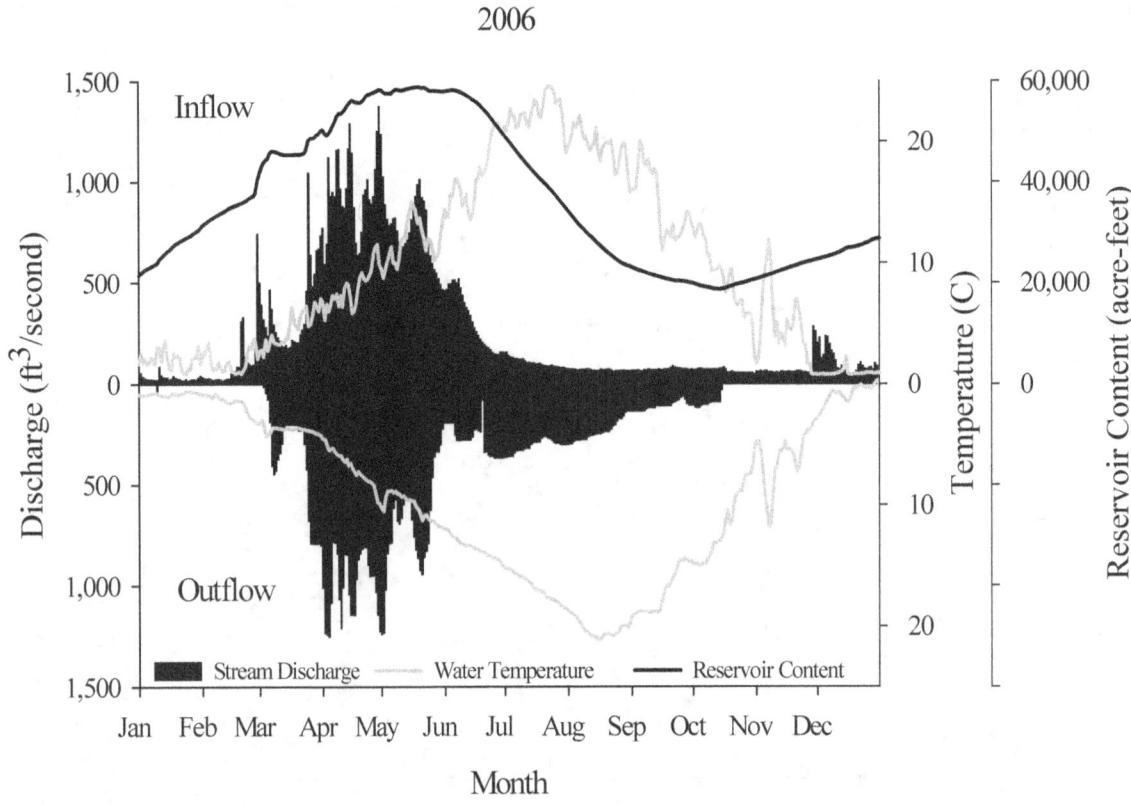

Figure 4. Inflow, outflow, and temperature of water entering and exiting Beulah Reservoir and reservoir volume during 2006.

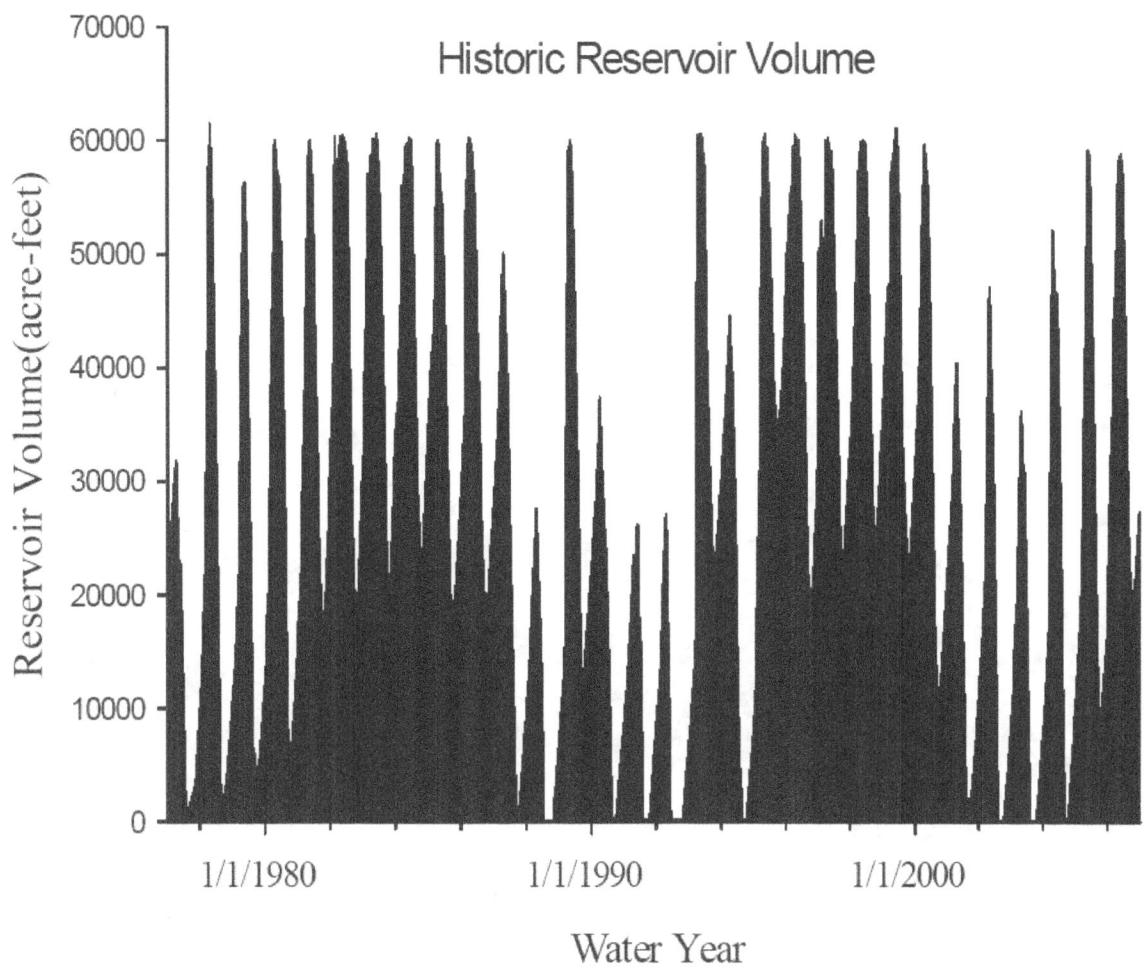

Figure 5. Historical daily volume (1977-2006) of Beulah Reservoir, Oregon.

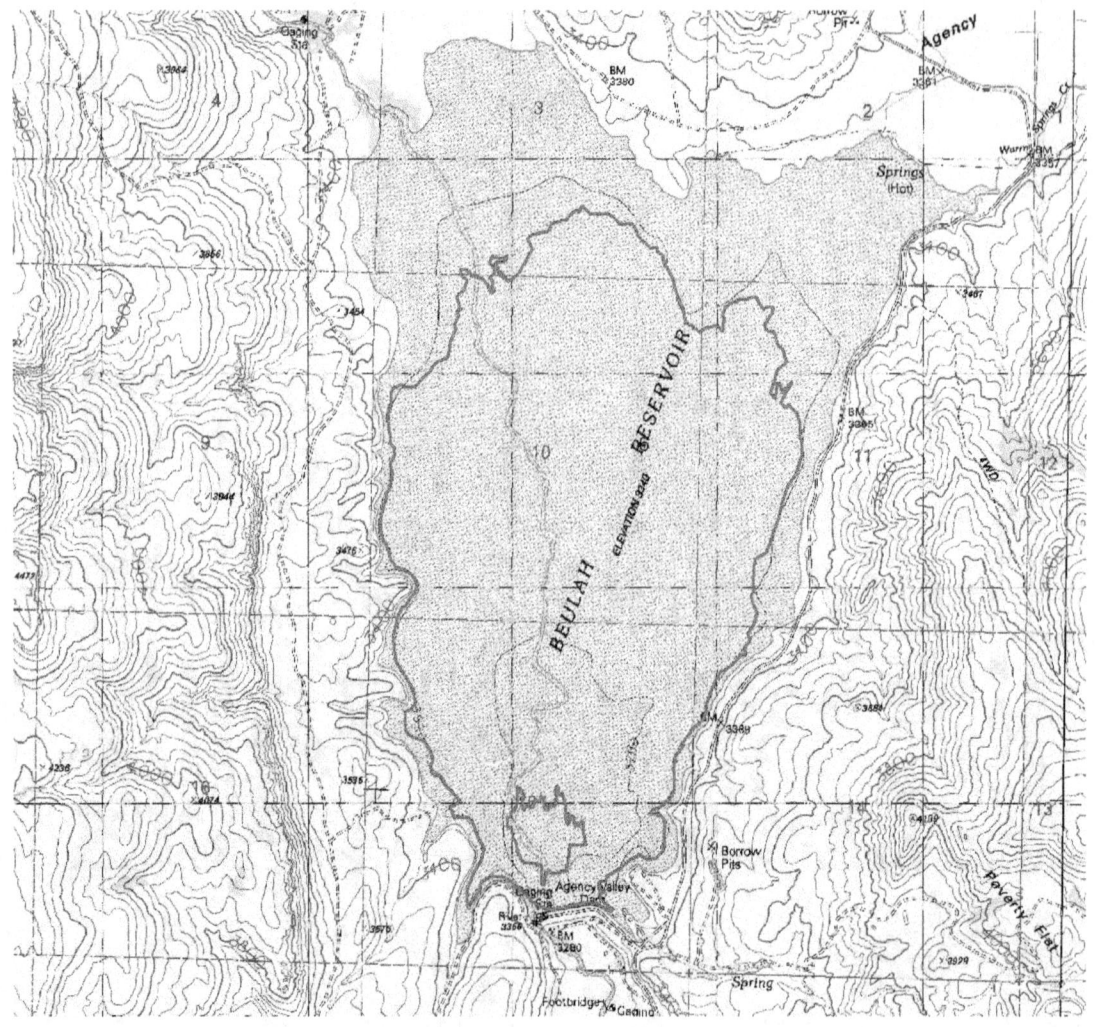

Figure 6. Locations of reservoir strata used in the collection of macroinvertebrate grab samples. Strata were defined as frequently dewatered (greater than1,010-m in elevation; shoreline to outer red line), occasionally dewatered (1,010 – 997 m elevation range; area between red lines), and generally not dewatered (less than 997-m elevation; area inside inner red line).

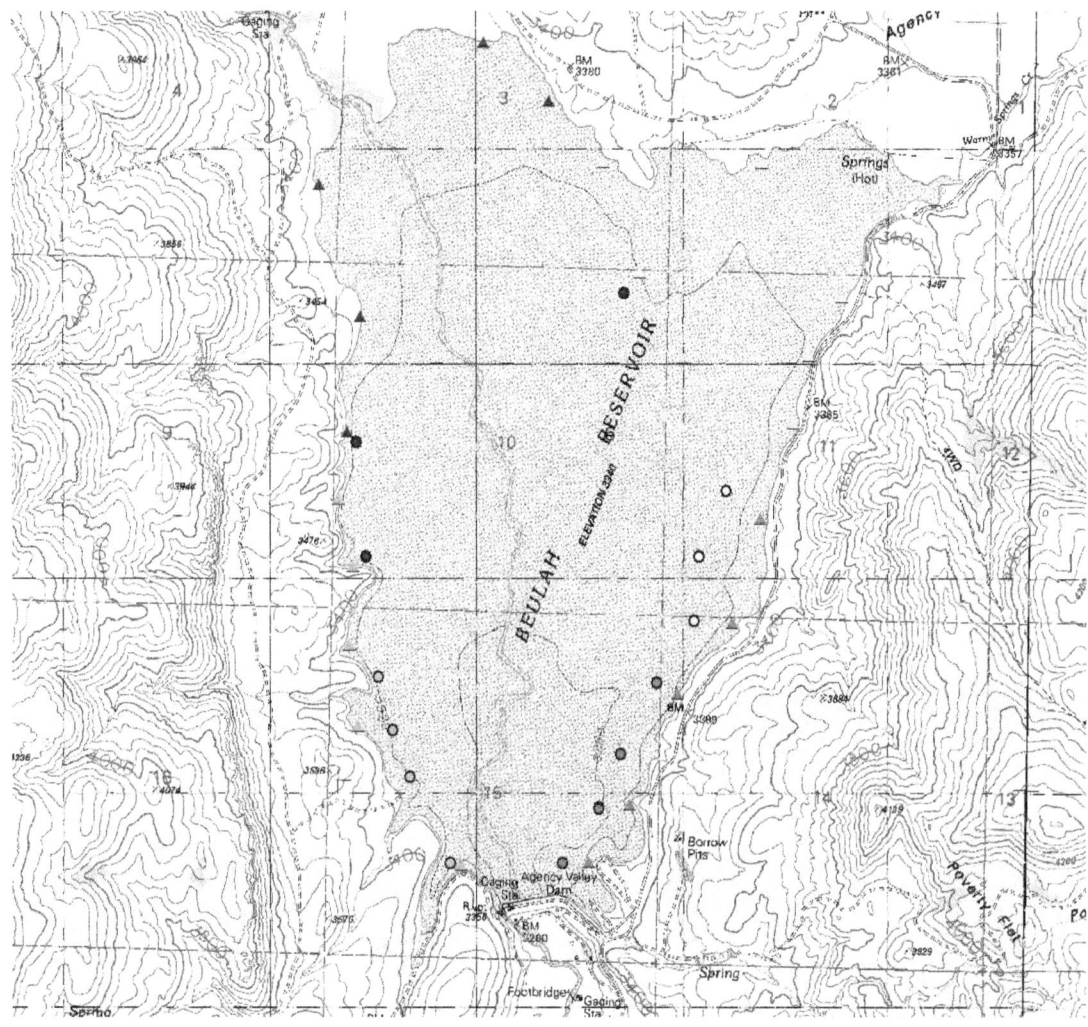

Figure 7. Locations of fyke net sampling on Beulah Reservoir during the spring (triangles) and fall (circles) of 2006. See the study methods section for a description of how sampling locations were selected.

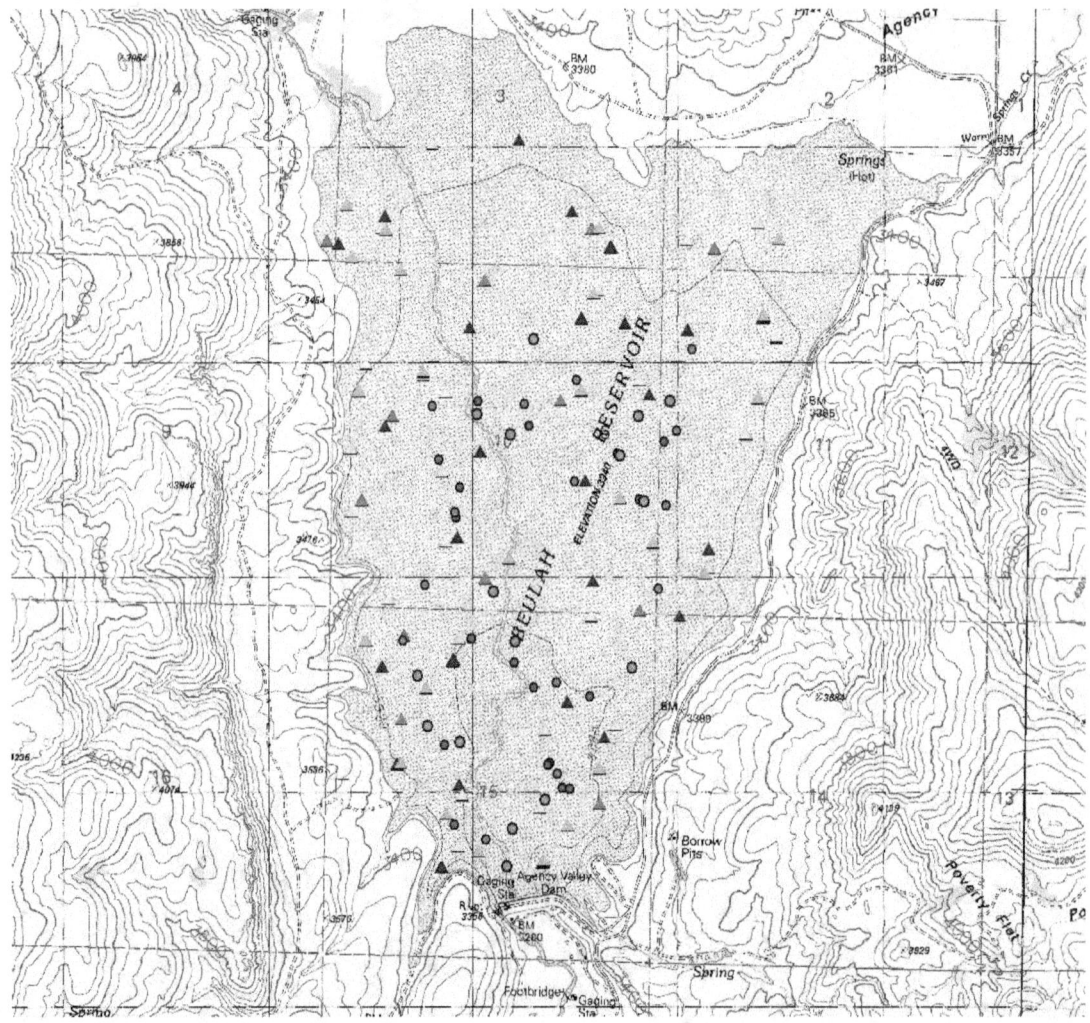

Figure 8. Location of gill net sampling in Beulah Reservoir during the spring (triangles) and fall (circles). See the study methods section for a description of how sampling locations were selected. Identical colors indicate nets were fished in the same two-week sampling period.

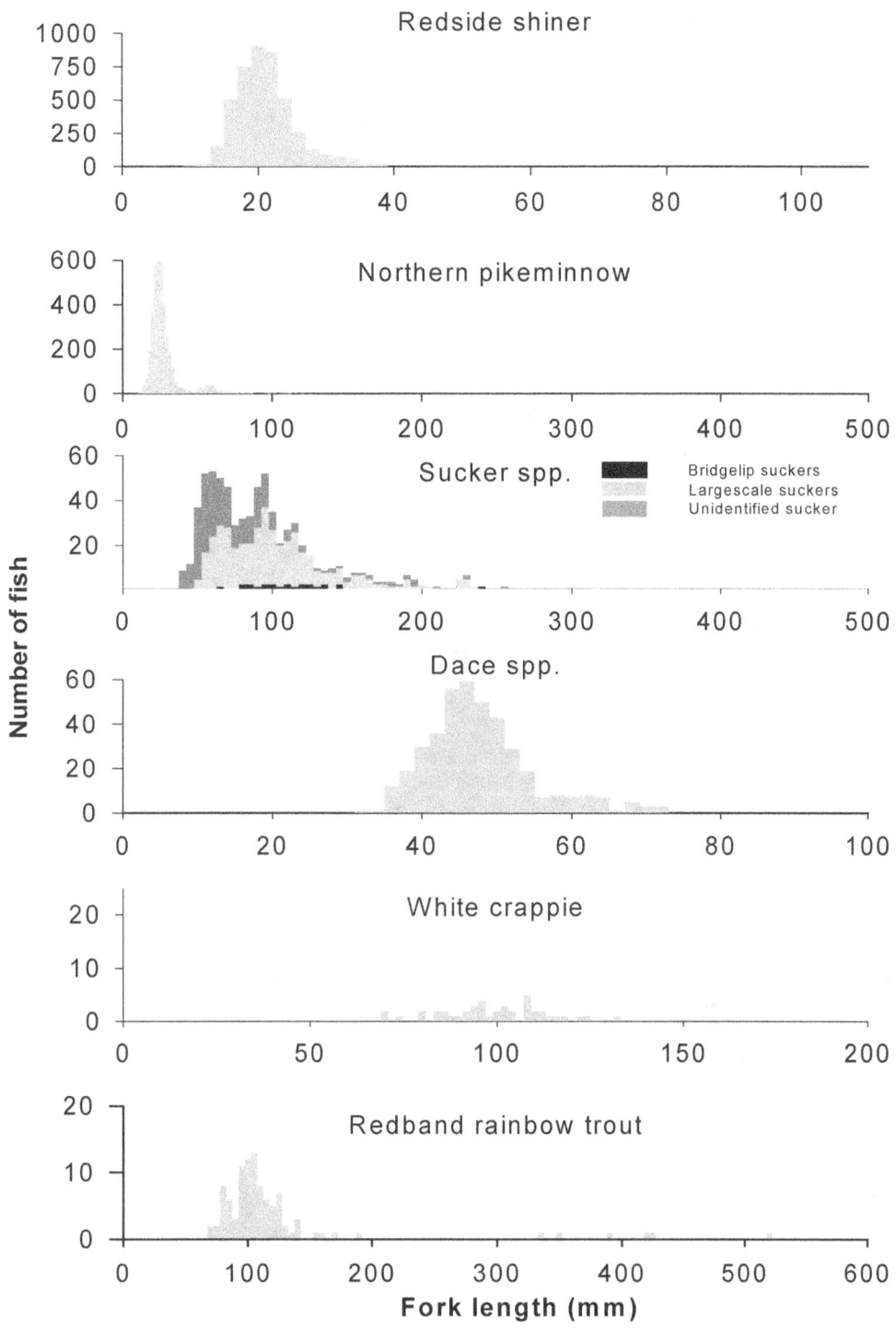

Figure 9. Length frequency distributions of fish collected with fyke nets in Beulah Reservoir during the spring, 2006. Note the different scales on the y-axis of some graphs.

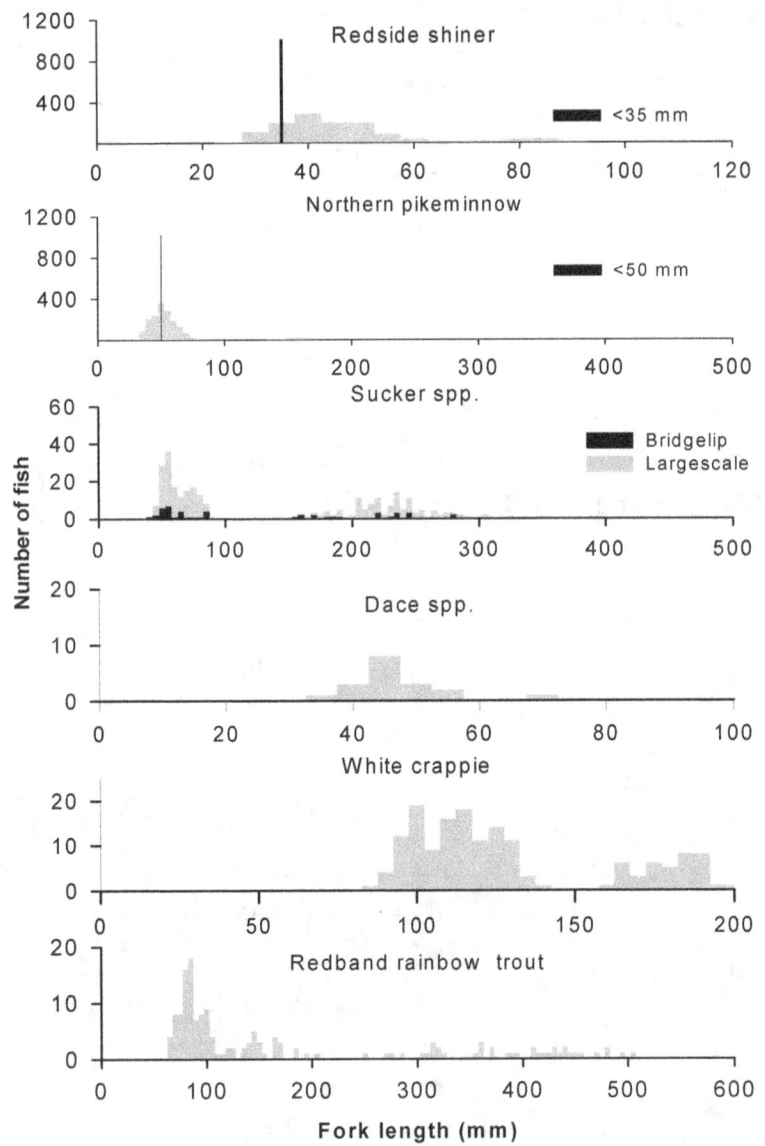

Figure 10. Length frequency distributions of fish collected with fyke nets in Beulah Reservoir during the fall, 2006. Dark bars on the northern pikeminnow and redside shiner graphs indicate fish counted by size groups and not measured. Note the different scales on the y-axis of some graphs.

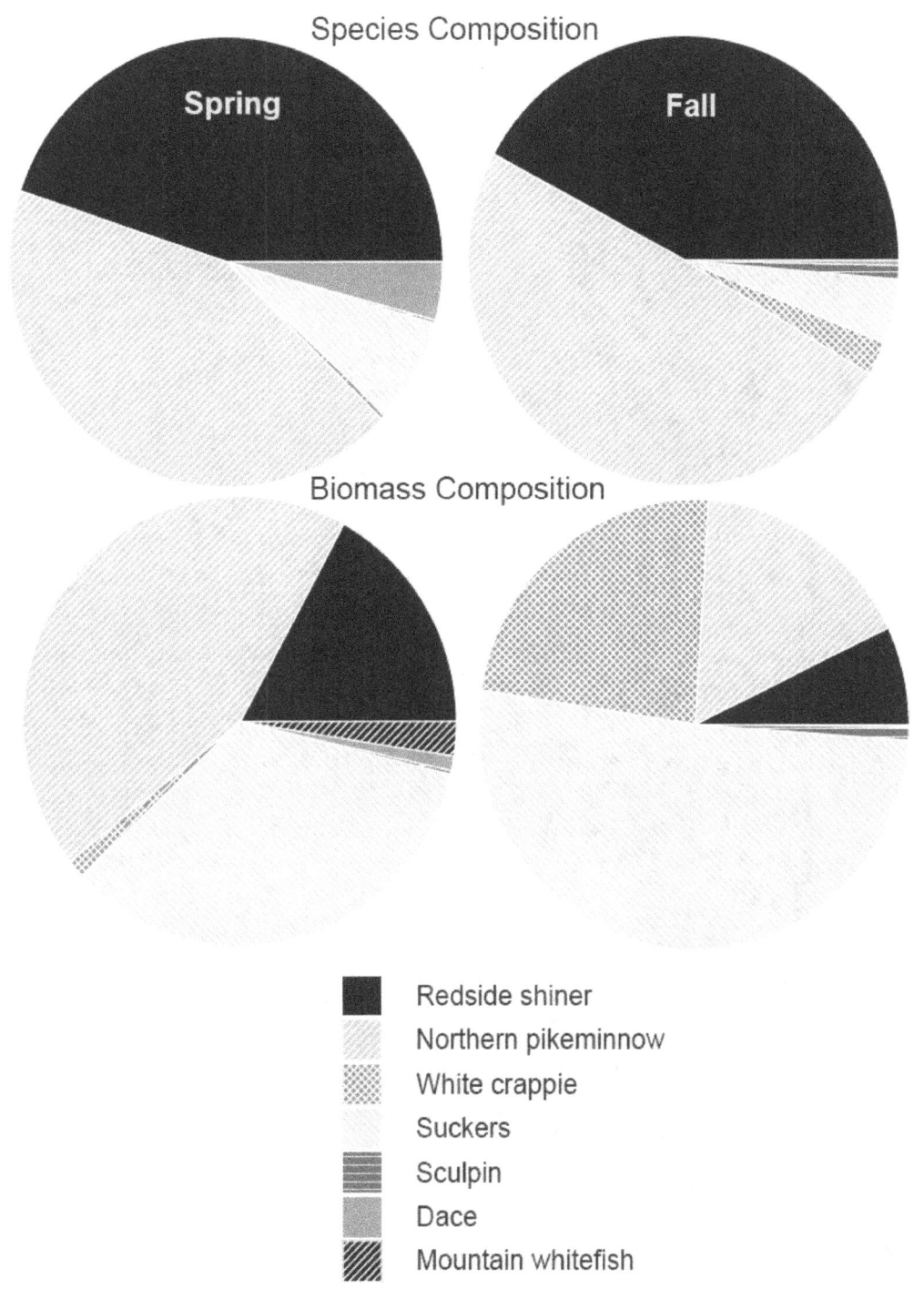

Species Composition

Spring **Fall**

Biomass Composition

Redside shiner
Northern pikeminnow
White crappie
Suckers
Sculpin
Dace
Mountain whitefish

Figure 11. Percent composition by number and biomass of fish collected with fyke nets in Beulah Reservoir during the spring and fall of 2006.

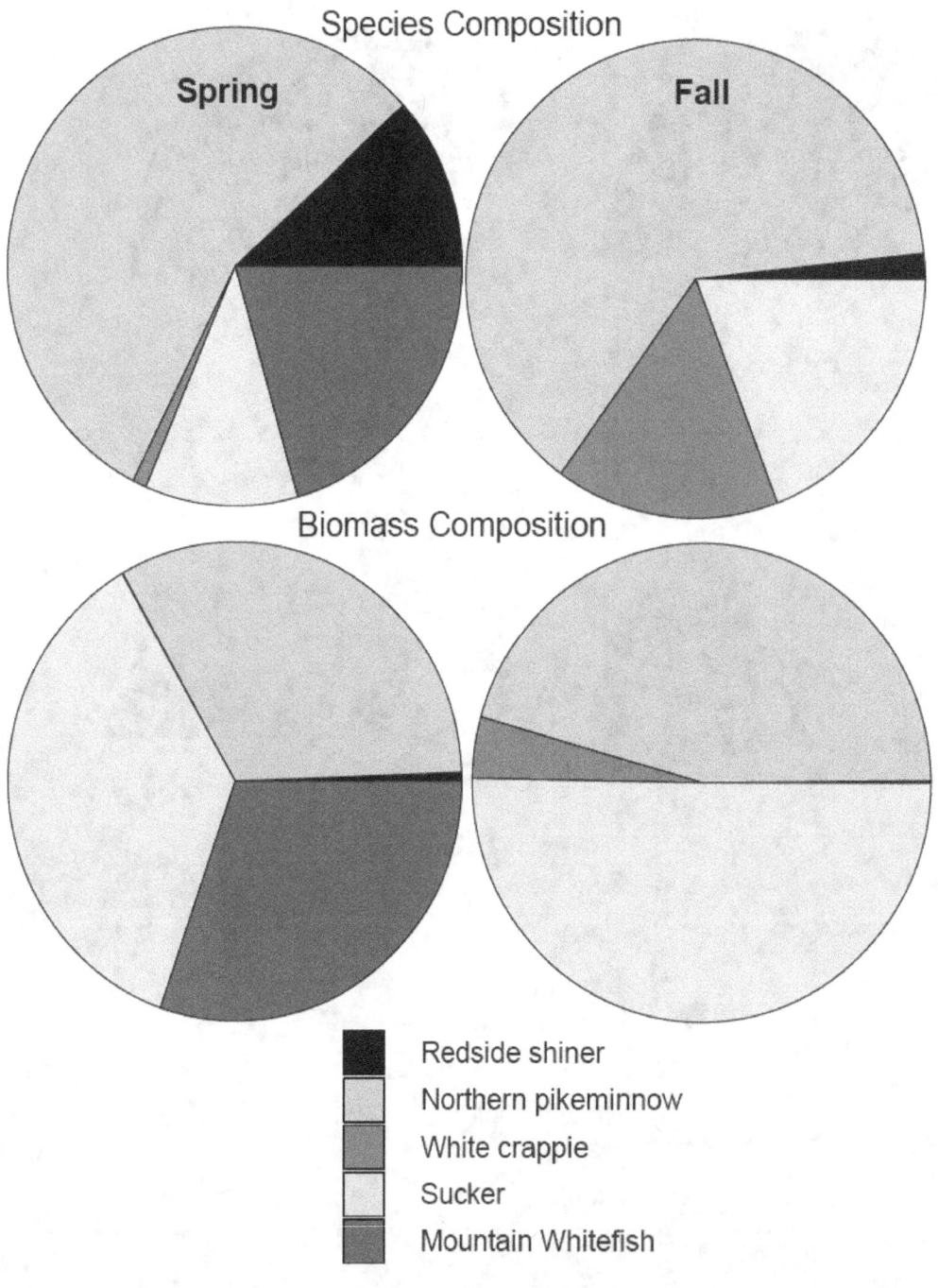

Figure 12. Percent composition by number and biomass of fish collected with gill nets in Beulah Reservoir during the spring and fall of 2006.

Figure 13. Beulah Reservoir when it was dewatered (top two pictures) and at full pool (bottom). The top picture was taken from atop Agency Valley Dam facing north. The bottom two pictures were taken from the head of the reservoir facing south.

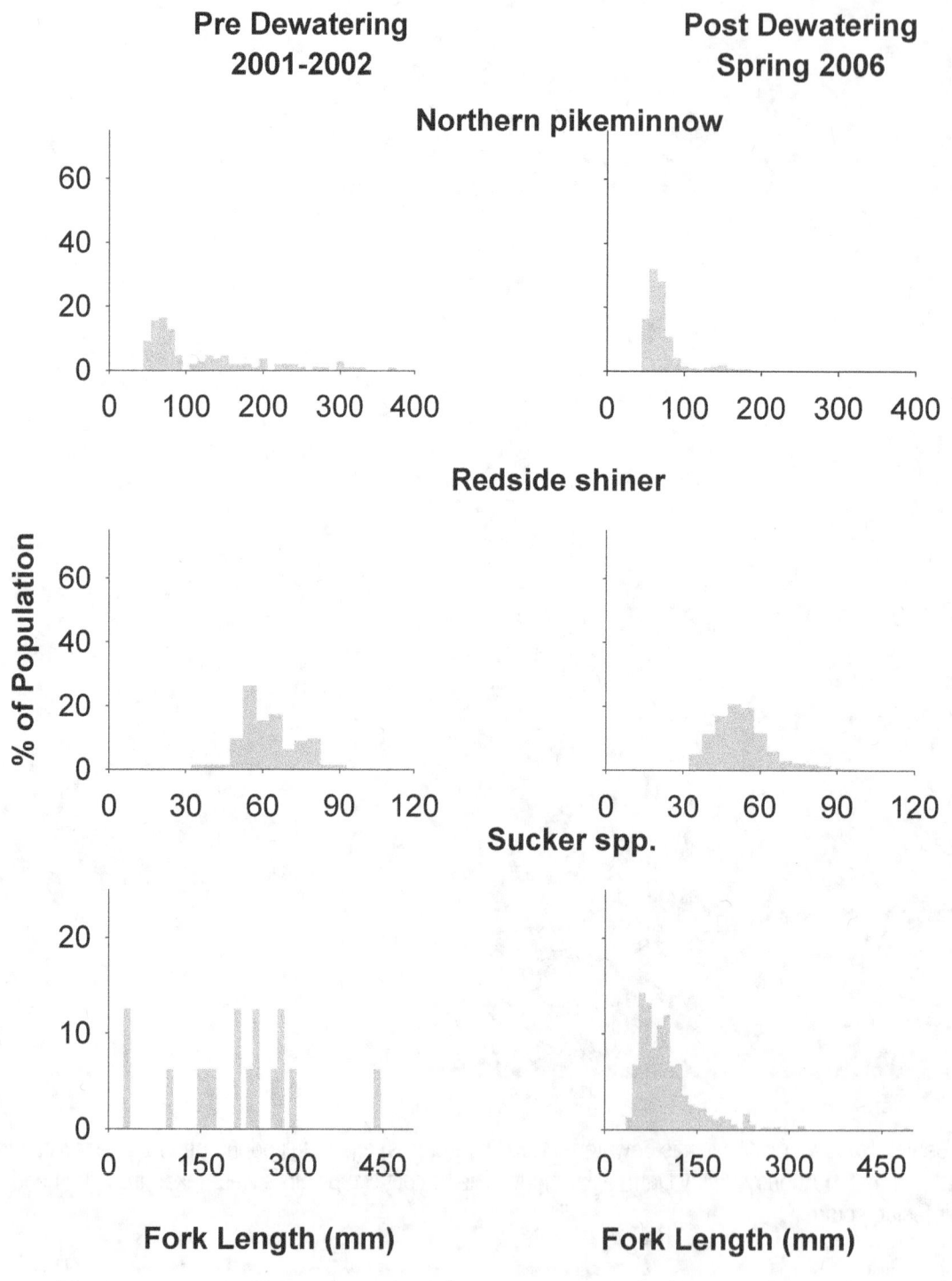

Figure 14. Length frequency distributions of fish collected from Beulah Reservoir during the springs of 2001 – 2002 and 2006. The reservoir was completely dewatered in 2002, 2003, and 2004

www.ingramcontent.com/pod-product-compliance
Lightning Source LLC
Chambersburg PA
CBHW080345290526
45791CB00009BA/2742